ANNE ASKEW
ON THE
KAFKA MACHINE

Barbara Smith

Barbara Smith

Anne Askew
on the
Kafka Machine

First published in 2020
by The Black Spring Press Group
Suite 333, 19-21 Crawford Street
Marylebone, London WIH IPJ
United Kingdom

Cover design and typeset by Edwin Smet

ISBN 978-1-913606-02-2

WWW.EYEWEARPUBLISHING.COM

For Finbar and the Furies

Barbara Smith
was born in Dublin and grew up
just over the North of the border. In 2005 she was chosen
for Poetry Ireland's / Éigse Éireann's *Introduction* Series. She has
an MA in Creative Writing (Poetry) from Queen's University,
Belfast. In 2009, she received the Annie Deeny Prize. She has
been a prize winner at Scotland's Wigtown Poetry Competition
and has been shortlisted for The Poetry Business pamphlet
competition and the Basil Bunting Poetry Competition.
Other publications include chapbooks *Gnosis* (1996)
and *Poetic Stage* (1998); and poetry collections
Kairos (2007) and *The Angels' Share* (2012).

TABLE OF CONTENTS

AUGUST HARVEST

'The wages of sin…'

An August day blistered
in latent asphalt heat.
Sister and I messing
in the back of a parked car,
our mother in the butcher's
across the street.

The car shudders
a low booming rumble.
Mother watches
the shop window flexing
inwards, sees the soldier
stumble, clutch his red
neckerchief and crumple.

I saw the tractor deflate
like the letting of air
from a space hopper.

Mother came back
revved up the engine
and left the square.

SHARP GROUND FROST

The moon lies broken
as smatters of glass beside
the tin can hulk of a car.

It's cold, bone cold as I
scrunch across the courtyard
of memories, cauled

in a reflection pool.
Glass glints catch the eye's
peripheries. This is no place

for a snail's trail, gone cold.
Safety has fled into the smear
of moonshadow. Blow cold

east wind in the neap of spring;
tide to the imperfect puddle
of remembrance.

POKER FACE

Here we are,
back at the beginning.
We sip and talk
genialities.
Then

... shark's fin,
glides neatly
beneath the rim of alcohol,
denies ever it was there,
dares me to define,
                 despise,
                      or ignore.

Shall we deal in words,
you and I?
I will cut
         the
             deck
                 3 times.
You will deal the charms
at arm's length.

Soon
we shall fall
tumbling through
a pillowed future,
back set against the past.
You shall see my hand
and I shall watch your downfall.

NOSTALGIC BLANKET

Today is blanketed in grey velvet silence,
all are caught in this twilit hour
between death and life. The land itself
waits for the imperceptible turning of the year.

We dull our senses, overindulge our heathen
ancestors. A time for thought sunk deep
in armchairs before flickering images
cast forth from empty vessels.

We are caught in the cotton of waiting.

DEATH OF THE INNOCENT

Their sun-strewn bedroom hazed
with the scent of exhaled alcohol,
tiny dust motes spiralled, caught
in the slanting shaft of sunlight.

Grandma was gone to early mass.
I had gone into their room
in search of breakfast, a small child
lively and artless in large volume.

Grandad huddled in the many-layered
marital bed. Above the brown-barred
bedstead, a picture stood:
Edwardian starch, patricians
ceding triumph to the future.

Grandma returned, suited and gloved.
                              I told her:
'Grandad won't wake up!'

Her eyes snapped shut like tomb slabs,
her face curious in its closedness.
'Here,' she said,
'have a bowl of Rice Krispies.'

What sound is remorse: the heavy tock
of the mantel clock, or the faint popping
of the rice in milk?

JESUS

was crucified
in my back garden.
I know! I've seen the
tall wooden cross withered
by sun, rain and age – and
the lines they stuck in
to feed him juice
when he was dying.

'I forgive 'em,'
he cried,
'for all their sins
I've died. I took it on
myself, to do this in memory
of you all.'

No-one ever heard that
conversation;
but the pylon remains,
steel and wood – there it is
without complaint.

OF SPUDS

After Heaney and Kavanagh

My granny used to soak the spuds
making it easy to peel them later.
Part of morning's ritual was topping
their pot with water. Later, after
fowl were fed and tae and bread were ate
she'd peel them slowly, humming all the while
a medley of Moore's *Almanac* songs.
Steeping my potatoes now, as she did,
brings her 'Four Green Fields' down the years to me.

Scaly and red, my Roosters. Instead of
her soft Queens, mine tattle of tractor harrow.
Long scars that I smooth away with a stainless
peeler. I split them with a long broad knife,
rinse them down and leave them by for dinner.

FAMOUS NUDE BY PICASSO

Today, I point two firm melons
at you. You latch on, voraciously,
pike baited.

       Later, I let you begin
fine-tuning, looking for your
favourite signal coming through...

But then, wanton takes over,
turns us about, directs things awhile.
Furious porphyry almost wholly
out of grasp.

Then we went home
and had a nice cup of tea.

NAMESAKE

Song for Sinéad

Through winter's mild softness
I cozened your weight within
waiting for this new production.

My heaviness grew that spring
your life quickening in my bulge.
I removed your father's ring.

The birth day arrived like others:
the gorge-deep gouging as
you were pushed into life's passage.

Finally you burst forth
furious at your eviction.
I marvelled at your newness
and named you for
Crazy Jane.

TEACH DUINN

A divided house of holding — Skelligs

Did they come to their rock,
Maighdean-mhara, to be wedded to yours,
bonded by the fate of the crossing?

The elder ones would watch the younger struggle
with interest: 'Here comes another who has
not loosed the bonds of stock and stone.'
                                        'He will learn.'
They nodded their assent as the heads hoved,
scaling Jacob's stairway shouldering parcels
like a betrothal of guilt.

And you Maighdean-mhara, watched, detached,
sun basking on your glistening galleries,
the foppery of men — tied to their rock.
The seasons washed you by, then the seasons withered.

Expectant you waited. They fixed stars
in the firmament, saw the ebb and flow
as the crux. You notched the rock,
kept account — God's ledger.

Now the stench of your filial friends
long since fled scourges your mind:
transfixed in the present,
chained to your rock, in counterpoint
to theirs.

MAGGIE'S FARM

H–Block hunger strikes, circa 1981

I remember well the weeks of dying,
thronged funerals held in pouring rain.
We huddled in our house and hung
black flags out because we should.

Maggie was not for turning; 'Crime is crime is crime'
was her deep analysis of the vexing occupation.
Besides, she would rather wage a war
in the South Atlantic seas. Another chance
for her to drum the chant of politics
and win her several years in Britain's
sinking sun.

Thus we westered in the haze of the setting empire.
Some would bide their time and negotiate history's
peace without the sound of gunfire. But yet
we wait... ages pass...

Parties polarize opposing forces –
those who pause for other Maggies,
impatient for the endgame.

RADIO HAMS

Tonight just doesn't make sense.
I have tried to listen carefully
to mangled truths; I'm tuning in

to my own warped wavelength
once again. You have tried too;
patience with an untried phrase –
a dead-reckoning is what you prefer.

We are tired now of trying and
so the conversation begins
for real. I tell you moribund tales
and you laugh: 'That can never be

as long as you are here with me.'
Still I am unconvinced by darkness
and the smell of summer turning
in the wake of our betrothal.

GRACE NOTES FOR MY PARENTS

You're angry again:
I can tell — silence drips —
muzzled rain too disgusted
to fall whole.

I have learned to read
pitch perfect tones, scale arpeggios,
orchestral scores that strike chords
of nothing.

Misery oozes through
the breeze blocks of my bedroom.
Gazing at the blind ceiling,
I wonder who offended who?

Now frustrated rage filters
through; one voice raised —
the other weeping, discrete
in its crescendo.

Resolution waits on
another night.

THE CRUMBS OF A PRUDENT HOUSEWIFE'S YEAR

After Dylan Thomas
Being kept and re-used to make stuffing for the turkey!

When the thieving hands of time steal back
What the tilt of the seasons has lent,
When the dim twilit hour fades in our hearts
Insistent the chime of old Chronos' song.

When the cook's thought turns to humble pie
And tender stewed meat and barley soups,
Then you know truly that winter is come
All toil of the year is the tale in the broth.

When the lackluster light of dreary doom
Calls the blackened kettle to hale good cheer,
'Tis then all good folk give greetings and say
'You won't feel it now 'til Christ's mass is near.'

EXTRACTION OF A SMITHY

An iron forge once stood beneath the playroom floor
in the heart of Clonalig, where once a smithy's anvil rang
hot metal under pound. The flicker of his measured
blows spark-skewed and he was caught in a life pulse
that winter's day.

'The locks here,' he murmured across the temporal plane, 'open to
another set of keys. You'll have to learn the trick by taste.'

I spent years at books and learning to understand
the ways of words and how they could tame men.
How my kin's blood twisted this tongue
around those keys and my mind learned
to forge a path from metal and become
a thoroughfare of thought.

I wonder, did those craftsmen clear the mind
as they raised the hammer in servitude to song?

I desire to strike my name upon this page
as surely as those blows, and know this inscription
will last a thousand years or more beyond the meaning
of words lost in the flow of lingual change.
But I am just another branch of the family of the smith,
doomed as all the others to be grounded into dust.

PAIR BOND

After Alan Gillis and Dolly Parton

The talk in the bar lulls a half-time fill:
as I knife-scrape the head from another pint,
he hovers, pocket-foothering his change.

Steadying for the ask, he addresses
my full frontals, my baby buggy bumpers,
my Brad Pitts, my boulders, my billabongs,

my squashy cushions, my soft-focus bristols,
my motherly bosoms, my matronly bulk,
my Mickey and Minnie, my Monica

Lewinskys, my Isaac Newtons,
my snow tyres, my speed bumps, my Tweedle Twins,
my milk-makers, my Mobutus, my num-nums,

my Pia Zadoras, my Pointer Sisters,
my honkers, my hooters, my hubcaps, my hummers,
my Eartha Kitts, my Eisenhowers,

my God's milk bottles, my Picasso cubes,
my chesticles, my cha-chas, my coconuts,
my dairy pillows, my devil's dumplings,

my objectified orbs, my über-boobs,
my one-part Lara, my two-parts globe,
my skywards pips, my lift and separate,

my airbags, my feeders, my mammy glands,
my Bob and Ray, my big bouncing Buddhas,
my sweater stretchers, my sweet potatoes,

my rosaceous rotors, my trusty rivets,
my melliferous melons, my mau-maus,
my tarty, my taut, my pert palookas,

my jahoobies, my kicking kawangas,
my agravic gobstoppers, my immodest maids,
my Scooby Snacks, my squished-in shlobes,

my cupcakes, my soda breads, my bloomin' baps,
my brilliant bangers, my brash bazookas,
my windscreen wipers, my Winnebagos,

my wopbopaloubop, bopalous,
my yahoos, my yazoos and yipping yin-yangs,
my paps, my pips, my pommes-de-terres,

my pushed-up, plunged-down, paraded balcony,
my slow reveal, my instant appeal,
my décolletage, my fool's mirage,

and I watch him pay up, steady up and leave.

A RARE OCCURRENCE AT GLENBEIGH

For Finbar

We leave the sulky atmosphere in the pub
and start for home up the steady incline.
Moonlit breakers thrum on Rossbeg strand
back-grounding our own huffing up the hill
and a shower dampens off the moonshine,
speckling our rain-cheaters and our spectacles.
A breeze gathers up the mist, pulls in white
light, like a Nissan's main-beams – but this light
doesn't corner country roads. Instead it builds
a slow parabola up through the air, sharpens
in moonlight 'til it arcs from sea to strand –
a lunar rainbow that lifts our dogged steps.
Just as swift in forming, it diminishes,
and thread-needle rain resumes its skirmishes.

THE PLIED PIPER OF DUNDALK

The door bangs open and he is whooshed
in by the cold breeze. He straps on his pipes
as quick as his arms emerge from coat sleeves,

cane concertinaed by another pair of hands.
His fingers itching with the tide-pull of music
that called him to the pub. He feels for the keys

glowing with a slow build, pouring heat
into the notes. They fizz like fireflies
into the hazy swirl above the other session players,

careening, bouncing off the ceiling, faces
turned, jigging elbows and swinging feet.
His new girlfriend curls in beside him, eyebrows

arched high, hair scraped skull-tight.
Does she fuel his urgency as he plays
an orgy of reels without raising a bead?

After music, a break. Now their cheeks glow
off each other's voices. Switched on, like sensor
lights, their skin fades when they face away.

THE WISH DOLL

I begged her to make it: the rag doll pattern
beyond me in a *Woman's Weekly* pullout.
An arm's blue outline reached over the centre page
to mitten hands, no fingers for opposing thumbs.

We decided on yellow hair, kinked
from ripped-out knitting; a shaggy fringe
cut across with black dressmaker's shears.
I plaited it; each strand took a child's age.

Its pert pink mouth was sewn shut. A pursed X,
and her eyebrows matched as sisters, not twins:
brown back-stitches on thick biroed lines.

I dressed it in my old kilt, a narrow waist
cinching a red bouclé t-shirt and tied on worn
dancing pumps with black laces, criss-crossed, tight.

CATTLE CRUSH

The yearling stores were gathered in the paddock,
'Go on'd' and stick-goaded into the yard

and routed narrower again, a ragged line-up
along the concrete wall behind the hollow bars.

First in line had no idea. He'd stick
his head into the crush-gate's yawning breach,

a blue cord clamping the grab arm tight to his neck.
Then, wedged to the wall, pincers reached in

for the soft, swinging 'u' below his muck-flecked rump.
Quicker than an eye's blink he'd be freed, bucking

off the white-hot pain in the field, he'd bawl his anger
back at my father swearing at the next one ducking in.

FEEDING THE CALVES

I have on my yellow boots to walk
beside your greater green ones. Our feet
splodge across the mud mouth
of the shed gate where the calves tread
muck and straw into an earthen brown
pocked with their cloven prints.

Even the rain has given up this winter.
The insistent chill invades my red anorak.
'We have wind from the North,' you mutter,
'that means snow and more blessed misery.'
You pour the calf nuts into the clang
of the metal feeder. A smell like warm tea
oozes from the calves' steaming breath,
as they nudge their heads through
the bars, warm in themselves.

ON NOT SEEING INSIDE THE SISTINE CHAPEL

You were a sky-gazer, a cloud watcher,
seeing within those steamed puff-pillows
the forms of fabulous beings.

Just now I saw a fisherman, his white head
turned away, his finger flung
behind him, pointing at infinity.

His rag-rolled head streamed to the west,
clothes rippling in a high sky-wind.
And when my lazy eye looked again,

he morphed into a huge ornamental 'E,'
whose top lintel was a crocodile's mouth,
snapping at the blue. This too bleeds,

feeds into sterling pound sign. You
too must have spent afternoons on your back
gazing at patterns forming and merging,

dissipating where the mind dragged it.
You took your pigments and pulled them,
your art fixing a borderless sky inside

a broad high vault, peopling the heavens.
Ah, Michelangelo, I know why the sky
became your backdrop, why you loved shades

from azurite, to smalt, to cobalt blue.

THERESA OF THE ECSTATIC UPLIFT

'Well, if that's divine love, I know all about it.'
— *Chevalier de Brosses*

I want to break with gravity's pull;
I crave consummation and mutation.
My folds blow inside out this intense
desire. It's not easy fixed to a marble cloud
companioned by that angel, his loaded
arrow, aware of coins slotting out a light-ray.
Anyway, who believes this idée fixe?

Beneath my eyelids is what you want to feel,
fluttering visions rolled up tight, re-arrayed
inside the deep folds of my clothes,
my toes curled in sacred shock, my tongue
slack against my mouth's roof, staggering
for Christ eternally, pulse chilled to stat —
betrayed by the integrity of stone.

They weren't trying to hold me down
as they grappled the dew on my hem
each time I climbed the cell walls,
my lips mumming long prayers,
ears tuned to some other colour
beyond the arid browness of Avila —
they were trying to rise with me.

Somebody succeeded though
in marbling ecstasy in deep creases.
Someone knew how to make my habit
textual, how to make coarseness
fresh and how to leave me dressed —
my face, hands and feet polished slick,
effusing from the erogenous zone.

STRETCH
After Roethke

Now that the earth tilts back to summer
and dusk dawdles late into evening,
we watch the yellow's sink to orange
across the broad shoulder of the TV.
Wooden blind-slats are flipped to dim the bright
harshness of what will only hold for three
or four weeks. Outside, butty, hacked-off limbs
raised to the sky – a neighbour's ruined tree
missing buds, cut far too late in winter.
I wait out spring's lengthening stretch
watching for night's first twinkle in the sky
as the day's clouds flee inland with the wind –
that slow dark that widens every eye –
it won't deepen until the long month of July.

BECAUSE I HEARD ABOUT THE HARP

I lived within the blast of barley tendril steam,
a hoppy smell, with hints of roasted grain,
as regular as the shifts that worked the clock.

Huge glass panes shielded copper tuns
from the purple gaze of Slieve Gullion
at the end of the train track that ran

on into the Gap of the North and up
the frilled green valleys to no-surrender-land.
Up there students drank it by the bucket;

down here, we called it Harpic and swilled our bellies
full in Russell's Lounge as Echo & the Bunnymen
belted our weekends into submission.

The question then was could it quench a thirst
as cleanly as it might after a salt-blue cycle
down the Navvy bank – my stomach knew

no better – wobbling back up tidy streets
of red-brick houses yielding sun-baked eddies,
abandoning a racer in a dim AOH hall

and pulling out a table and four chairs
to a sunlit square no bigger than the table;
how daft we all were, long before Diageo.

ACHIEVING THE LOTUS GAIT

In winter, the uphill path to Madame Xing's
is treacherous. I watch for loose
stones among the grey brown gravel

and the birds are almost silent
as each step quarries me,
wincing on wooden pattens.

Madame unravels yards of stinking cotton
from my feet and her thorough thumbs
knead them from numbness.

She honours my feet with warmed water
loosening shedding skin,
trims each bruised nail to the quick.

She rebinds each foot in cotton lengths
soaked in herbs and animal blood.
A neat figure-of-eight turns

over instep, gathers toes, under foot
and round the heel, each pass tighter
than the last. And then my thoughts

cringe homewards, as I totter out under
a brittle moon; my own weight
crushing each foot into the correct shape.

SUMMITING

You must know the end to be convinced
that you can win the end, cool and quiet:
the solemn dome, fine and firm above all
its chasms of ice, its towers and crags,
this thing that all your desire points up to.
Here experience distils the muscle ache
and crystal skies into a bleary memory
of how you gained the top in so many days.
The conquered enemy is but ourselves.
Success means nothing here. Kingdoms of rock,
air, snow, and ice, we hold for just the time
it takes to survey in a slow circle,
soberly astonished by our struggle
to master mountains with our own flesh.

KNITTING SERPENT

Entranced, I used to watch your work
stretch on clicking pins of steel.
One day you taught me how to hold
the twist and make my own work grow;
she took the twine
into darkened recesses,
wandering wildly;
but I was always dropping stitches
that unfurled into gaping holes.
Carefully you'd unpick my work,
start me again and off I'd go;
from season to season,
looking back always
to trace the twisted cord's progress;
you made me make my own school jumpers.
I came to dread July's dead heat,
knitting up the bargain yarns
just in time for school's return;
there was no end, no beginning
to her searching, groping blindly;
Jane saw all ways but remained mute;
later, came complicated patterns:
cable, moss stitch or basket weave.
Your tricks taught, correction made,
my new repertoire outgrew yours;
tongue-tied in the web of fine twist,
her fingers grasped,
still aching to reach the end —
I yearned to stretch beyond your patterns,
faking up the antique designs,
yet you insisted on your stitches
knitted in the dullest twist;

the centre, the eye of calm –
there only
the shattered symmetry;
      long since, after you unravelled
      I still complicate time and stitch;
      no threadbare yarn, no knots entangled –
      tongue untied by wordy skein;
blood moon radiant,
fingers crooked behind;
there wasn't much left to see.

ALICE'S BOUDOIR

I watched you
at your dressing table
through the looking glass.

Your left hand lifted
the silver handled brush
and you began to sing
as you brushed
down the years.

I longed to copy you,
look through your eyes.
Carefully you softly
brushed dark tresses,
coyly eyeing yourself
as dim light encroached.

You only ever turned
your back on me once,
when you gently
placed the brush back
in the coffin at the
end of the bed.

INVENTORY

The scatter of our stores at base camp —
neat wood crates enclosing rows of tins:
herring, peas and beans, soi-disant 'fresh' sardines,
Heinz spaghetti, sliced bacon, Hunter hams;
biscuits, Ginger Nuts, Rich Mixed, tins of jam,
sauce-bottles for Mess, brandy, whiskey, gin;
an impressive heap of Yak's dung, and paraffin
in large green and blue metal two-gallon cans;
thirteen Europeans in monogrammed
fleece-lined moccasins, long Jaeger socks,
their armour of wind-proof cotton smocks,
finneskoes, hob-nail boots all revamped;
and sixty porters in English underwear,
leather jerkins and puttees from Kashmir.

ICARUS' REBUKE

After Cohen

If I could ruin my feathers in flight
before the sun went down in its mad blaze
don't you think that I would try, Father?
I have that part of you that you forget
the thrill and whirl of air's soft element
caught and hooped inside your homespun wings —
not just the plodding plot of movement,
the means of making good our long escape.
I am the payment that you will make:
the interest owed on science for your art,
the fall from joy that cannot be recaptured.
I know you warned to steer a middle way
between the sun's ambition and water's douse,
but not listening is what youth does best.

LUCIFER TAKES A BREAK

He stirs sugar into black, watching white crystals
transluce. He rolls a cigarette, crimping a white tip
and dark tobacco carefully within the rustle of thin
paper and remembers, as he snaps a match lit,
a time before: just an instant.

There was darkness there, but warmth.
Yes, gorgeous warmth... a 'shh' pressed
to his lips before he was handed down.
The whisper of white noise... voices?
He remembers, how long the fall was, how sheer, how short.
He sips the coffee, thankful for its bitter sweetness.

WILD FLOWERS FOR RUTH

After snow and rock,
to see things grow again
as they like growing:
enjoying sun and rain – that is real joy.
I collected a bunch of wild flora:
pink cranesbills, yellow cinquefoils,
plants that looked like our violets,
grass of Parnassus, which I really love,
and a brilliant pink button flower,
which I think may belong to the garlic tribe.
Most of all, I found kingcups,
a delicate variety, smaller than ours
at home; somehow especially
reminding me of you.

NEW START

Each day happens as it has before:
one starts in crisp, sunny air by eight
and walks for a good stretch at the start;
say half-a-dozen join up in the chore
of tiffin and later we flog our hordes
of beasts the last miles to our encampment.
Generally, our enormous mess tent
precedes us and awaits us, all footsore.
A usual – and by now welcome – sound blast
in each place is Strutt's voice – scourging
this march for being more dull, cursing
that village for being more filthy than the last.
He's not a grouser; he just likes to ease things,
like his feelings, with these maledictions.

TINY YARN

Quickly, fingers curl and arch
around steel needles looping yarn.
Casting stitches on, she murmurs
the pulse of each one, purling

a matinée jacket selvedge
and counts the tens in French –
dix, vingt, trente, quarante, cinquante –
as her eyes follow the current.

This is how she knows to love:
a complex pattern in pale olive
emerging from her tapered hands.
She knits past the screeching qualms

of postpartum blues, the hissy-fits
dispersing into fan-lace stitch,
reaching for the calming rhythm
of knit one, drop one, slip one, knit one

and turns each row gradually to length
that measures a slow unclench
back to a sleeping shape that lies
in a Moses basket, by her side.

CAVATINA

A recurring dream

You have withdrawn to the heart's cavern
of mahogany and floral bedroom carpet.
Your things make a centred pile: a keyboard
of grained rosewood, a box of yellowed scores,
a folding music-stand – a defiant pile of last
importances. You have a plan for living
but you are short a few thousand pieces
to make it turn to gold. I hear you out,
ask you for more details. You shrug as though
'Never mind those – see the quality, the weight.'

This is where I always turn away from
what cannot be avoided – yours or mine –
the losing of our shadows, the loss of song,
the long leaving up Jacob's ladder to home.

MIRROR IN THE BATHROOM

After The Beat

Locked in the bathroom at twenty to eight
you battle against pustules and wiry cow's licks
with creams, gels and sprays – a shield as you quit
the house in a stink-haze of mumbled sub-bass.
Each zit leaves blueing scars, adult skin growing in.
Later, your body shot with growth impulses
you gorge on toast and apples, half a chicken –
or carve bored skin slits across your forearm.

Are you Narcissus wielding a mobile,
thumbing swift-boot texts to a sullen Echo?
No. You are not him: no rosy-cheeked youth
staring down at your image, no knowing who
you love more than another's cosy glow – you've
that same self-doubt we've all waded through.

SPECULAR EFFECT

It's bad luck to centre
yourself between
two mirrors

to rear your view
check the jean's cut

and see your eyes horrified
by an infinity
of huge arses

LAST WORD FROM THE ARTS OFFICE

For fifteen long years I watched Market Square,
its cars and people on the way to elsewhere.
I was, for some, a haven of solace,
for those in the know, the 'other' ticket office,
or the means for artists and musicians
to grow into their muses. From children
on St. Patrick's Day to poets on Dundalk FM,
from Presidents of the USA to banjo-picking Chairmen,
I've seen them all push through my jingling doors –
even gave directions to large coach tours.
Grown from small seeds in a wooden shed,
huddled behind a certain man's shoe shop,
these small steps for arts have moved back home
to make footprints greater than walls will ever hold.

ANNE ASKEW ON THE KAFKA MACHINE

All night I lay under the itch of a dot-matrix printer,
stuttering a bleak message across my skin.
From fontanelle to toe, ink flowed into every pore.

I had become their text. They studied me for defects,
editing my mouthed pearls, passing into their ears
and on to old pages, old ink, old seals.

Then they showed me the machine, the angles of the frame.
They twisted rope about my wrists and ankles
and then they bound me, dialling up the message,

inscribing me with their sentence.
I dislocated, slipped bones from sockets without noise.
I bled inside before the needles finished

their tattoo, the soft infill where spine meets pelvis.
The sentence they inscribed? Witness.

CONFINEMENT

Four foot by four
from beam to floor
and wall to eave
leaves little ease

to walk or sit
or lie at rest
pace in your mind

CREWEL WORK

Pin brightness pierces
and drags the thread taut.

The pluck and thrum of stitches
stabs their own rhythm.

This is no pain-by-numbers,
the pattern pricked and pounced:

slit stitches sliver a lion's ribs,
the lamb's outline couched

in blended fustic hues;
all gently seeded with shadow.

Seven years in waiting:
filling, edging copes and mitres,

before a psalter's bookbinding
when her fingered vision fuses.

FUZZY DREAM MEMORY

Have you climbed the wooden hill to sleep,
or do you fall, all edges and sharpened angles,
letting light invade through door-cracks?
Only darkness lets the raw light inside.
Your closed eyelids pool it into forms:
people you have met, places you've never been.
There the furniture is fuzzy, faces younger.
You're allowed to wear your tears more strongly.

Are these the possibilities of other lives:
questions you couldn't ask, promises unmet?
Glimmering soul-ghosts tug your braided limbs
through the spokes of your own breaking wheel.
Copper-fastened, the rim will never run
as true as the old red blacksmith meant.

THE GRAND THEORY OF TURNING RIGHT

Along the drumlin roads of Cavan
your mind swims with potential's promise.
From the moment of conception we move
towards the place we started out from:
our cells vibrate, divide and grow;
we practise blindfold in the water-womb,
until life's urge pushes us towards
the air and warmth of waiting arms.
Still we seek motion as our hands reach
to pull water past our graceful curves,
moving through our lives, a slow arrow
pointing to who knows where, or what, before
we go. These narrow lanes have a habit:
they'll bring us back to where we all come from.

WHY OISÍN WENT AND CAME BACK

The night he left, a high, white arc bridged
the deep sea and the smooth strand:
a moon-bow, a mix of light and rain that allowed
her voiced cry to come to him, alone, beached.

Sea stallions waited for him in the keening surf,
dolphins, to carry him west despite a head's warning.
And did Niamh wait? How long, how very many years
of watching each tide rolling, each wave's weight

under stars and clouds? How much sea between
them? She always knew he couldn't stay enfolded
in the colours of their love. Too hard the bond
of living weighed on him, against the abalone

of her skin, the blackness of her hair.
Another night he came back across that rare
white arc that bleaches red and indigo to grey,
and saw her necklace laid in lights across the land.

THE TALLYMAN'S HARVEST

Why did you think you could cheat the tallyman?
Each day passes, brings new changes.
Your feet gnarly in your shoes; slowly the cloven hooves
seem to manifest. Each step begins carrying

you closer to an aching realisation,
the shaking of your body an admittance
of the nerves' shredding cores. The plaited twist
of yesterday's life shrivelling over time. Each thread moulds

to the bonds of love and life. What lies
within the brain? — That old cauliflower of
construction; the florets furled too tightly
for the grinding shattering of beeping machinery
to release the real secrets of spreading
degradation. The tallyman will have his dues.

NOTES ON POEMS

p. 4 'August Harvest': the subtitle is from the Holy Bible, Romans 6:23, 'the wages of sin is death, but the gift of God is eternal life in Jesus Christ our Lord'.

p.13 'Teach Duinn': In Celtic mythology, Donn (son of Milidh) was the Irish Lord of the Dead who made his home at the place of his death, Bull Rock just off the western coast of Dursey Island, Cork, and called it Teach Duinn (House of Donn). It was said that he could be seen as a phantom horseman riding a white horse across the waves, and the souls of his descendants gathered there.

p.13 The Skellig Islands are two uninhabited rock islets off the southwestern coast of Ireland. Some traditions place the House of Donn there.

p.13 'Maighdean mhara': sea maiden in Celtic mythology.

p.19 'Pair Bond': versions of this poem have been published in Barbara's collection *The Angels' Share*, Doghouse Books, 2012, and in *Catechism: Poems for Pussy Riot*, English Pen, 2012. It has been performed many times with the Poetry Divas all over Ireland.

p.30 'Achieving the Lotus Gait': this poem was shortlisted for the Basil Bunting Poetry Competition, 2009, and was also published in *The Angels' Share*.

p.31 'Summiting': previously published in 'Mallory Sonnets,' *The Angels' Share* and in *Southword* Issue 18, 2010.

ACKNOWLEDGEMENTS

With thanks to my family and Eyewear Publishing.